A Successful Woman's Handbook:

Social Networking for Women in Business

Building your Business Profile and Connecting with Your Customers Online

Monica S. Flores

A Successful Woman's Handbook:
Social Networking for Women in Business

For more information:
http://www.asuccessfulwoman.com

ISBN: 1-4404-2035-1
ISBN-13: 978-1-4404-2035-1

Printed in the United States of America
October 2009

Dedication

Dedicated to all of us, working together, who make a positive difference in the world.

Let's take care of each other, learn from each other, and build up bridges of understanding.

Plug in and find others who are committed to building up a world filled with love and light.

-M. S. F.

Preface

This second book in the "A Successful Woman's Handbook" series helps you navigate through the many different tools available to communicate, collaborate, and join forces with like-minded individuals who share your interests.

The purpose of this book is to give you concrete information and step-by-step tips on how to build a valuable professional social network online.

I encourage you to use data reporting and analysis to measure your results after implementing the following tips.

In the spirit of communication, honesty, transparency, and integrity, I invite you to connect with me directly by finding me online: a search for my user handle "monicadear" will go directly to my pages.

Monica S. Flores
September 7, 2009

Contents

Acknowledgments

My love goes out to my husband for being my partner, supporter, and coach.

Special acknowledgments to Susan Gunelius of Women on Business and Apple Levy of The Green Girls for giving me opportunities to share my thoughts through frequent articles.

Introduction

Social networking is poised for exponential growth, fulfilling the trends predicted long ago (or was it just a few months ago?) for people to find their primary tips and sources of information, recommendations, and referrals from other people they like and trust.

For many women in business who grew up in a more private and "trade secrets" kind of environment, today's trends fit the typical "Millennial Generation" outlook. In this approach, which is based on open, collaborative, highly transparent and group-focused relationships, our challenge as business owners is to think about, understand, and incorporate into our business practices the focus on "We" and team instead of the focus on "Me" and myself.

This book lays out the basics of what you need to successfully grow and utilize your social network for your business.

Use the book to learn more about existing tools available. Plan your social networking strategy and get tips on how to make the most of your limited time online.

Chapter 1: Social Networking Basics. Understand the basics of social networking and some ground rules that you'll want to incorporate into your online activities.

Chapter 2: How to Connect. Step-by-step tips to integrate your online connection process with your offline and in-person networking.

Chapter 3: What to Post. Find out how to build your network so it is valuable to you and to others.

Chapter 4: Etiquette and Maintenance. How to make sure you remain gracious, calm, steady, and supportive to your growing network of fans, friends, followers, and connections.

Chapter 5: Expanding your Network. Use optimal search terms and key phrases to find other individuals that share your interests.

Chapter 6: Measuring Data. Use metrics to understand the "big picture" about your online persona.

Chapter 7: Final Tips. Find additional expert tips to make the most of your social network.

The ***Resources section*** contains step by step details on Facebook, LinkedIn, and Twitter profile setup, as well as my own contact links.

I use these tips in my own professional networking, and I'm confident that the methods here will sharpen your ability to be a trusted resource to your clients, friends, and associates. Grow your business by sharing your knowledge and building your community of clients through social networking.

Here are a few questions for you to consider about your current social networking strategy:
- Is it working for you?
- Is it sending you qualified leads?
- Are clients and customers finding you through your social networks?
- Do you have the ability to "keep up" with your profiles?
- If not, will you allow someone else todo it for you?

Remember to consistently learn and improve, fine-tune your approach, and review your results every month.

SOCIAL NETWORKING DETAILS:

Key Phrases to describe your business:

Link:
Username:
Password:
E-mail:
Notes:

Link:
Username:
Password:
E-mail:
Notes:

Link:
Username:
Password:
E-mail:
Notes:

Link:
Username:
Password:
E-mail:
Notes:

Link:
Username:
Password:
E-mail:
Notes:

Link:
Username:
Password:
E-mail:
Notes:

Chapter 1:
Social Networking
Basics

- Your Social Self is not your Real Self -- or is it?
- 1. Preparing: Get your Data Together
- 2. Content is Key: 5 Questions to Answer
- 3. Simple is Better: Boldly Go Forward
- Summary to Keep in Mind: Stick to the Basics

Your Social Self is not your
Real Self - or is it?

I encourage you to do periodic searches on your name to find out what other people see when they seek out more about you. How do you feel about the top ten search results that display?

Are they rants? Embarrassing photos? Links to something discomfiting or salacious? Tedious paperwork that you forgot you put online? Does a Google or Yahoo! search on your name turn up mostly good links about you, such as white papers, authored by you? Blog posts you've authored? Guest interviews or podcasts?

Your very first impression, in many people's eyes, is the first few results in a search on your name in Google.

To manage that "social self," which is a construction of you in the online world, you'll want to bring it as close as possible to the "real you" that does business in your particular industry.

If you're a radio show talk host known for ranting, then you want your top search results to be rants. If you're in the embarrassing photo business, then yes, make sure the top results for you are definitely those kinds of photos. However, if you need to project a more professional image, or if you need to present information related to your field or industry, I recommend you use all the tools available to you to increase your profile. These tools include socially shared links, blogs posts, podcasts, PDF's, websites, photos, reviews, and profiles, all highly searchable by your name or company name.

Your search results have a great chance of increasing the likelihood of someone wanting to do business with you and your company.

If your results are not as expected, consider ways to increase positive search engine results related to you, such as increasing your authorship of articles on a blog, uploading more pictures tagged with your name, and increasing the publications, announcements, events, and testimonials related to your name.

In the tips in this book, we'll go through a step-by-step process to increase your profile. Your first step is to get an assessment of your online persona today. Then, in the next few months, use these tools to manage your profile.

Tip 1

Preparing - Get your Data Together

Your name is a unique property on the web as much as it is a unique identifier for you and your business. Claim your name by registering it on any and all social networking sites that you intend to use.

If you have a name that's common, consider incorporating your middle initial, a nickname, or unique user "handle" to make your online persona unique. I use the handle "monicadear".

Consider registering a domain name (like janedoe.com) for less than $10/year at a domain registrar like GoDaddy.com. You can always decide where you're going to point it -- if you don't yet have a website, a Wordpress.com blog is an excellent first start.

Going to http://www.wordpress.com and registering your name or user handle will give you a free blog such as http://yourname.wordpress.com. Next, forward your domain name to this starter blog and start "padding out" the blog with page content related to you, your company, and your values. When anyone types in your domain name, it points directly to the blog. This is a great way to have a starter website.

Other social networking sites where we recommend our clients register include, in prioritized order:

LinkedIn.com
Facebook.com
Twitter.com
Delicious.com
Wordpress.com
Flickr.com
YouTube.com
FriendFeed.com
Yelp.com
SlideShare.net
MySpace.com
Gravatar.com
Blogger.com

As new services start to become available but you're not yet ready to start filling out your profile on that service, at least "claim your name" by reserving your username, and return at a later date to fill the profile out. Consider opening up a "ClaimId.com" account where you basically reference yourself and your multiple links in one place: Here's a sample version of my own page: http://www.claimid.com/monicadear

A working e-mail is essential for all of these profiles. Set up a Gmail account (Google Mail) as a primary "catchall" for your social networking-related profiles. Alternatively, consider using your work e-mail, but forward a copy of all e-mail to a Gmail.com account -- you may always use this as your archive. Keep in mind that if you leave your current job, you may not be able to access your work e-mail, so I recommend you maintain a profile that is unique to you and all your work experiences, not just one job.

Checklist of website pieces for your quote:

☐ Personal name you intend to use
Business name you intend to use, if different

☐ Headshot of you, or logo at varying sizes

☐ E-mail address, recommend Gmail.com

☐ Personal description

☐ List of keywords to use when creating your personal description

Tip 2
Content is Key:
5 Questions to Answer

In your social networking outreach, as in your business, the quality of your profile is what drives interactions. Be as niche-specific and direct in your answers as possible.

Five Questions to Know about You:
- Who are you?
- What do you represent?
- Where are you found online?
- How does your company help customers?
- Why do you do what you do?

As you organize your social profile, provide clear and concise answers to the above questions. Your answers are typically searchable, so as you answer the questions, be specific for the most informative profile. Your results may be more easily matched to those who are seeking you and your unique skill set.

By directing people to your business or personal website, you always provide a way to have people follow up with your core business.

Consider the overall objectives of your social networking endeavors. For me, it is to keep in touch with varied people I've met over the years, to maintain connections as time passes, and to meet new customers, supporters, and associates.

Checklist for your content:

☐ Keywords identified and used as guidelines for posting

☐ Posts always mention some combination of the following: Who are you? What do you do?

☐ Where are you? When are you available to help me? How do you help?

☐ Why should I choose you?

☐ How do I contact you?

☐ What's the next step to doing business?

☐ How do I learn more about you and your company?

☐ Posts are relevant to one of the above?

Tip 3

Simple is Better: Boldly Go Forward

Stumped about what you'd like to talk about in your "Twitterstream"? Not sure what to place on your Linkedin profile? Don't know what to share on your Facebook status? Keep it simple. A quote has been attributed to Eleanor Roosevelt - "Great minds discuss ideas, average minds discuss events, small minds discuss people."

Discuss ideas. Discuss research, original work, trends, insights, and your assessments. Discuss results and lessons learned from recent projects.

What I've found in my own research and in working with clients is a typical progression that goes like this:

A) You start by posting basic thoughts (like what you had for dinner, or what event you're attending, or something you're shopping for)

B) As time passes, the quality of posts and the type of topics you'll post about becomes more complex

C) With more comfort and a regular routine, posts become more topical and match your ongoing blogging or product/project update schedule

D) As you become more professional in your approach, you use tools like CoTweet.com, Twitterfeed.com, Feedburner.com, and RSS feeds to "seed" your social networking profiles with content related to your business: some of this may require additional expertise to set up.

E) You develop relationships with others who are interested in the same issues you are: find these people through a search on your specific keywords.

F) You develop a consistent schedule to keep your profiles updated -- and you stick to that schedule.

I recommend you hire a social networking specialist to keep your company profile updated if you don't have the capacity to do this in-house.

Alternatively, do "group" posting, where multiple people are responsible for one official company account.

Summary to Keep in Mind:
Stick to the Basics

As you develop your social networking profile, there is no rush, and there is no need to feel like you must "pad out" everything on your profile all at once.

For early adopters, you've already claimed your profile at most of the sites and you are able to "play" by learning more about how to use these tools. For those who are just getting started, take advantage of the infrastructure that others are building: for example, people joining Facebook after their friends have the ability to receive "friend suggestions," reducing the need for an intensive search.

As you develop your online profile, prepare your information, including your contact information and main keywords. Answer as much as possible about your business, such as your website, goals and objectives, programs and services offered, and how to contact you.

A main idea to keep in mind is to keep your social profiles simple. You are using these tools to create a cultivated network of contacts. By keeping things simple, you provide direct and accessible ways to reach your customers and client base.

Why bother with a social networking profile if you are not going to use it to disseminate your own media, share your posts, connect with like-minded individuals and organizations, and build the web community?

Think of your social networking properties like you would think of your website: using these profiles are a way for you to connect with others on their own timetable, instead of through a phone call or in-person meeting.

Social networking and social media sharing are excellent tools to share and search for information. They also provide pathways for you to foster linkages with your core community. I like to call today's mailing list your list of "cultivated contacts." You begin with a very basic involvement, such as a Twitter follower, and you can always move your contacts up the "chain of involvement" with you and your company through additional levels of engagement.

Having someone start out as a reader of your posts or as a follower is a good first start.

Chapter 2:
How to Connect

- Why Connect? Reasons to Build your Network
- 4. Share it: Your Signal-to-Noise Ratio
- 5. Create it: Original Research Matters
- 6. Recycle it: Re-posting Information
- 7. Answer it: Your Knowledge is Valuable
- 8. Talk it: Offline and Online Efforts
- Summary to Keep in Mind: How to Connect

Why Connect?
Reasons to Build your Network

Utilize your social networking channels as a way to connect with others. You may use these avenues to produce information and share stories: by doing so you gain trust, earn referrals, and encourage "buy-in" from your potential customers.

Here are five reasons to build your network:

1) Increase the overall knowledge of your field and industry. Help people ask the right questions and they'll be more prepared to work with you and your associates.

2) When you give away, you receive back: we've given away hundreds of pro bono hours and we continue to receive referrals and partnership opportunities because of our outreach.

3) Increase the links associated with your company name or personal name and increase your page rankings in search results. Make your name synonymous with your area of expertise.

4) Make use of technology to assist everyone within your particular circle of influence: social networking allows those in your network to interact with others in your network. You never know what kinds of connections may arise from friends of friends.

5) Sharing is a tool of power: when you give away your knowledge, you build your reputation, which converts to client confidence and trust in your integrity.

When you find ways to share your knowledge online, you build your business and your personal reputation.

There are many ways to increase your authority in a field, but sharing your knowledge online and in person is, in my experience, the best way to dominate your niche sphere of influence.

One good way to check if your social networking efforts are paying off is by doing a search on your specific keywords. If one or more of your profiles appear in the top ten results, you're doing well.

Tip 4

Share it:
Your Signal-to-Noise Ratio

I like to use social networking profiles to find other people interested in my particular field of interest and to share tidbits of knowledge with those specific people.

While everyone wants more followers, and there are plenty of products that promise X number of fans, what is most helpful to you are targeted, interested users that feel a connection to you and your company.

We can learn from Vin Diesel, whose Facebook fans page has over 5 million users (as of September 2009). In a smart display of savvy and connection, he posts videos of his home life, Facebook-only entries and pictures, and messages through his discussion boards. The people on his Fans page receive information "straight from the source" without mediation from CNN, YouTube, a PR agency or the film distribution company. The people on "VinBook" feel a deep connection to the actor directly. You'll see more and more public figures using social networking channels to develop a direct relationship with their fans in the next few months.

As a guideline, I write a blog post approximately three times a week, and each link gets posted to my Twitter and Facebook Fans page. I also maintain connections with people on both my friends and followers list-- if I'm connecting with someone, they are connecting directly with me: there is no "robot" or "auto direct message" that is associated with my account.

My personal relationships are currently separate from my "work" relationships. I do use Facebook to keep in touch directly with friends from elementary school and former jobs. However, there is some crossover. If you anticipate using your social networking profile for business, consider opening a separate Fans page or Group dedicated to this process.

Continue to treat the other people on your lists as real people. Everyone is hungry for real communication: that's why people check their e-mail, check their Facebook page, and check their Twitter direct messages. Connect on a personal level and feed this need.

Tip 5
Create it:
Original Research Matters

For postings, I encourage you to come up with original research that relates to your work.

In general, any kind of original work that you create is worth sharing within your social network profiles: this includes books, articles, widgets, downloads, coupons for products that you sell, and opportunities that you're offering.

Examples of how you may post original research include:

- a graphic designer might create an illustration or graph that helps explain current trends in the news

- a data analyst might crunch some numbers that are of interest in a particular field, like health care or business trends

- a topical expert might share the results of the latest research in the field

- a chef might share a few kitchen tips on keeping clean or prepping for a meal, or even a recipe or two

- a wellness practitioner might offer some physical exercises

- a professional might offer analysis into current trends and ways that people can prepare for the future

Consider the types of questions that people ask you on a regular basis. Is there any way you can offer information that will help your customers be better informed or make better decisions?

Information to be shared through your social networking channels includes anything that helps illuminate your business practices and sheds light on your company's approach to solving a problem, any products or services you offer for free or for download, any initiatives you're involved with (such as a charity drive), or news and events pertinent to your organization.

Tip 6

Recycle it:
Re-posting Information

From time to time, you may find the need to "RT" or re-tweet. Basically, this is the equivalent of forwarding. If you do intend to post someone else's original information, make sure to give credit where credit is due.

Recycling and re-posting information may take the form of the following:

Original poster Jane Garcia at XYZ Company posts a link to research from her company on business trends through 2010.

Secondary poster Angela Yee re-posts the link: "Forward from Jane Garcia: link to research from XYZ on business trends through 2010."

What a typical re-tweet looks like in Twitter would be: "RT @janegarcia research on business trends through 2010 http://www.link.com"

The number of re-tweets you receive is a good indication of if you are a content creator or a content recycler. If you find yourself consistently re-tweeting or re-posting others' information, consider developing a plan to create your own content and use that to balance out your output.

Many people are interested in what you have to share. When your posts are valuable to a certain, unique set of people, you will benefit that subset of people: seek them out as those are the people who will ultimately be interested in you, your products, and your services.

Anyone can quote someone else, but few people come up with original quotes. What can you come up with that's original, provides value, is educational or interesting, and makes a difference to your client and customer? Share it!

Checklist for your reposts:

☐ Is the posting informative, useful, or valuable? If so, repost it!

☐ Original poster is credited (refrain from passing off someone else's work as your own)

☐ Add some context about why you find the post informative, useful, or valuable

Tip 7
Answer it:
Your Knowledge is Valuable

Use your social networking profiles to provide answers and support to potential and existing clients.

For example, your Twitter stream is a great way to solicit and answer questions. Some companies use Twitter to handle tech support issues. Consider using your Twitter profile as a way to demonstrate your knowledge in your particular field. Your answers, if described in detail, will be picked up by search engines and will contribute to an overall search result on you and your area of interest.

Consider using a tool like CoTweet.com to manage multiple people posting to one account: I use CoTweet to schedule posts on multiple accounts (such as product releases or posts that mention my specific keywords).

Reserve specific proprietary knowledge for paying customers, but consider what you can share online for free, and use your tools to share answers.

Tip 8
Talk it:
Offline and Online Efforts

I highly recommend you go out, meet, and talk with other people. We cannot allow social networking to take the place of live, in-person networking.

Some examples of using social networking to support your in-person efforts:

• Attend any of the multitude of conferences or seminars in your specific field or industry.

• Create an informal meeting with Twitter or Facebook friends who are nearby

• Organize a charity drive and work with others in your social networking sphere to promote a local nonprofit or community-based organization

• Join a board or leadership group around one of your areas of interest -- invite the support of others in your network

• Promote an event that you plan on attending and invite people from your social networks

• Share with others who are interested in your specific topics -- take someone out to coffee or lunch to get to know them better

• Consider offering a seminar, panel presentation, or group review of a specific topic you'd like to explore

• Book clubs are great ways to meet others and come up with stimulating discussion - join or start one around an interesting book schedule

• Work parties are great ways to get together and support one another -- they can be physical or digital work parties - join with others to work collaboratively on a special project

• Party time: you can always host cocktail hour, supper club, or an intimate breakfast

• Choose your own!

The important part about getting together in person is the ability to foster additional connections that carry you forward.

Summary to Keep in Mind:
How to Connect

Connecting with others is the main point of social networking. Share your own expertise and experience. Talk about what you do best. Reciprocation is key: give something away, and you'll receive something back.

Create your own worksheets, white papers, articles, or checklists. Your research is valuable to others interested in your field. Use your research as a launching point for a conversation or to start a relationship.

Repost information, but make sure that repostings are meaningful or valuable to your readers. Always make sure to credit an original author. You are more helpful to your reader as an original thinker than you are as a parrot or echo chamber. Your original voice is meaningful, so share it.

Share your knowledge through answering frequently-asked questions, or do an "ask the expert" function where you answer specific questions. This is a great way to use the keywords that you would use in your work, and it is very helpful in the overall "search" function: your consistent use of keywords allows other people to find you and you to find others interested in the same topics.

Finally, remember to connect in-person with your virtual contacts. Face-to-face conversation encourages more trust, transparency, and relationship-building. The World Wide Web is here to support human interaction, not to override it.

Use the tools at your fingertips to encourage person-to-person connections. Realize that a Twitter or Facebook relationship is only one facet of the deep connections we make with one another --- and an electronic relationship is merely bits and bytes on a screen -- the true connection comes from ongoing relating, story-telling, sharing, and communicating.

NOTE: For those of you suffering burnout. Focus on what you love. If you feel overwhelmed by constantly "paying it forward," take a moment to regroup, reconnect, and refocus. Find a place of strength and feel free to say "no" to opportunities or people that do not directly fit your philosophy or field of interest. By specifying and being clear, you open up more targeted opportunities.

Chapter 3:
What to Post

- Be a Resource to your Customers
- 9. Links: Feed your Community
- 10. Ideas: Hash it Out
- 11. Events: What's Happening?
- 12. Values: Take a Stand
- Summary to Keep in Mind: What to Post

Be a Resource to your Customers

Customer love is your mission when building your business-- this means loving your customer and helping them. Use your social networking profiles to enhance your mission of generating customer goodwill, knowledge, trust, and feelings of connection.

A thrilled customer who "talks you up" to ten people is exponentially more valuable than a paid advertisement. On the other hand, someone who negatively rates your service makes your outreach so much more difficult.

Consider ways that you may provide resources to your customers to:
    A) solve their pain, or
    B) make their life better, or
    C) entertain, educate, or involve them.
Match all of your publicly-accessible social networking posts against that list, and as long as one of those needs is being fulfilled when you hit the "submit" button, you will be fine.

Become a resource and your customers trust you more: do this by sharing links, overall ideas, events, and your values.

Tip 9
Links: Feed your Community

The Web is a vast storehouse of billions of web pages, with terabytes of information available in any type of topic. Links that you promote through your portion of the World Wide Web will relate directly to your keywords and to your fields of interest.

Typical links include blog entries that you or someone else has written, breaking news, polls, downloads, and topics of interest in your field.

The trick with sharing links is walking that fine line between narcissism and information-sharing. Are you becoming too much of an egoist? Are your links too self-referential, or worse, are they abusive and spammy? Consider running your link through this checklist.

Checklist for your links:

☐ Is your link "evergreen"? Will it stand up to the test of time? Are you sure it's a longtime resource or are you referencing a passing fad?

☐ Is your link informative and educational? Does it help your customer?

☐ Is your link simply a commercial message? Be advised that posting relentlessly may earn you some snide remarks or "unfollows."

☐ Does your link provide more insight or information on who you are?

☐ Does your link provide information about what you value, or what you stand for?

☐ Is your link a repost? If so, make sure to give credit to the original author.

☐ Did you leave some context information about what you are linking to?

☐ Is your link original? Focus on your specific keywords for your specific business - keep your links "on-topic" and you'll find those links appearing on search results related to your specific keywords.

Tip 10
Ideas: Hash it Out

"Tagging" is a way to mark your content within a particular category or sphere of interest. People use "hashtags" to mark the content of their post and to make it easier to find through search engines. For example, Twitter has been an excellent search tool to find people in real-time, based on their tags. I use Twitter to find people who are talking about the same things I'm interested in.

For example, in my account, I've saved these searches:

http://search.twitter.com/search?q=minority+women+business

http://search.twitter.com/search?q=green+women+business

I periodically log in and run the search to network with or follow other people interested in what I'm interested in.

You may use tools like TwitterFeed.com to import your blog posts into your Twitter feed. You may also use the "Import RSS function" to feed your blog posts to your Facebook page. Each of your blog posts may be prefaced with a tag that describes the body of the post.

For example, the keywords I use within my social networking sphere include:

minority women in business
business
minority-owned
woman-owned
green
success-oriented
fair trade
organic
progressive
sustainable
eco-friendly
holistic
sharing
community
social justice
dream
vision
believe
achieve
create

I use topical keywords such as Drupal, Wordpress, PHP/mySQL, Joomla, OSCommerce, custom content management systems (CMS). These allow me to find others in my industry.

The point of tagging your content is to allow search engine functions to find it. Use multiple tags to help sort and organize your postings. You may also do a keyword search on specific tags. By searching on your specific keywords, you find others posting about the same things you're interested in. You may connect with others who are interested in the same topics in which you are interested.

I find a mix of postings between personal and professional can be helpful. While you don't need to have every single one of your posts be a "work" post, it does help if the majority of your content that you generate is directly related to highlighting and advocating for your specific point of view.

My rule of thumb is that at least 7 out of every 10 of my posts has something to do with at least one of my main keywords: the rest are more personal or topically directed to an individual or small audience.

Tip 11
Events: What's Happening?

Events are a great way to share your knowledge and to connect with others in your field. Keep abreast of events by subscribing to a Google Alert (http://www.google.com/alerts) in your topic area.

Large gatherings in your particular industry and smaller retreat-type sessions are the most valuable events to attend in real-life, as they are a great way to vivify your routine and to encourage you to connect with others in your field. Consider posting additional links to conferences, seminars, networking events, parties, and panels that you might not attend but would be valuable to your followers and friends.

Additional examples of events to post include speaker panels, conventions, book readings, work parties, volunteer opportunities, charity events, galas, fundraisers, retreats, general membership meetings, and personal appearances.

An easy way to manage this schedule is to use an online calendar to organize your own work schedule and post your links to that calendar page on your website.

Tip 12
Values: Take a Stand

We move people not by facts and figures, but by stories, epics, and tales. We describe information not through link after link but through graphs, pictures, and symbols. We connect with others not through marketing-speak or commercial language but through the sharing of our values.

When you are posting, resolve to always talk about your values -- these are what truly identify you and allow others to assess what it is you stand for.

If you do not yet have a values statement, operating principles, or a mission on your website, post it in a prominent place and refer to it often.

Your values are what connect you to other people. What do you value? What types of values do you embody in your personal life? What values does your company have "built-in" to its dynamic, customer communications, and product offerings?

Your values are important. Always keep them in the forefront of your mind and be active in talking about them through your web posts.

Summary to Keep in Mind:
What to Post

A good rule of thumb to consider when creating a post is this: **if it sounds too commercial, it probably is.**

While I have no problem when others sound like commercials, I advise you engage in this activity relatively infrequently. No one wants to see commercial after commercial in your messaging: people want to see "real" posts, not "fake" posts. I think people *might* be comfortable with your commercial messaging as long as it's tempered by an all-around sense of personalization, knowledge-sharing, and communication in your posts.

People want to connect with you and learn about what is important to you through the links you post, the ideas you explore, the events you're interested in, and your values.

When you post a note or link or promotion of any sort, run it through your personal self-promotion detector. How would you feel if you saw a post like this coming from someone else? How do you feel about having a permanent link to your post on someone else's page?

If you're comfortable with what you're sharing, post it. Request and invite feedback from others in your community. Use this feedback to "tweak" your marketing model a little more. Find the right ratio of messaging (between commercial and editorial content) that makes sense for your company.

Whole Foods is an example of a national brand using its social networks to reach out to consumers. Whole Foods uses its Twitter accounts to post local links, national news, and ongoing specials, answer customer support queries, provide links, and share grocery information. All of these postings are valuable to both customers interested in Whole Foods as well as others who may become customers with enough exposure.

Hawaiian Airlines uses novel social networking programs to connect with users. Along with a members-only login and password section on their site, they offer Twitter specials, Facebook Fans specials, and reminders of unadvertised fare deals.

Look to the brands you enjoy, trust, and appreciate to see how they integrate social networking into their approach. Use similar ways to connect with your own clientele.

Most people who are following you don't need the constant advertised specials: they follow you, or connect with you, or join your mailing list, because they want to know more about you and your business.

As examples:
• I'm a Facebook Fan of Big Island Candies, which offers gourmet chocolate-dipped shortbread. I love the mouthwatering descriptions of ingredients, the heartfelt president's message, and the design that goes into the catalog.

• I'm a Twitter follower of Skincare by Feleciai, an African-American owned luxury bath and body store, because the company is committed to creating a sustainable community that fosters self-care, health, and wellness for women.

• I'm part of the "Green" Linkedin group because of the information and resources that are available from other professionals on the list.

Consider if your post helps build your community. If it does, feel free to post it. If it does not, consider why you need to post, and do a little bit of assessment before you click "share this."

Chapter 4: Etiquette and Maintenance

Connecting means Showing you Care

We must always remember that social networking online enhances and enables our innate person-to-person connections.

The "search" function within Twitter, for example, has been so helpful for me because I find others who are specifically interested in my topics of interest. When you identify your main topics of interest, reference them as keywords or tags when you create your posts and links. You may preface a blog entry or link with a few keywords that explain what you are posting.

The type of connection you foster through your social networking efforts is the kind that is genuine and "backed up" by an in-person connection. It does you no good to have 100,000 people who don't care what you say. It is more important for you to identify those individuals who are deeply, passionately committed to the same issues you care about, and who share your mission, vision, or values.

Connecting with others is but one way to reach out and show that you care about your relationship with others.

Tip 13

How to Meet People Online and Offline

There are three ways I typically meet people: through direct contact, through a friend of a friend, and through a search in my chosen field of interest.

Direct contact includes both people with whom I share close bonds as well as people with whom I have connected in person.

Friend-of-a-friend relationships typically rely on the strength of the initial friendship and the trust inherent in referencing a mutual contact.

"Asking around" is an equivalent of the search function. I invite people in my network to give me references or referrals to particular types of people.

Social networks offer varying degrees of support for each of the above kinds of search functions.

Facebook connections are typically through one person who you know as a friend. When you add them to your list (or they add you), you are both acknowledging that you are each other's direct contact. You may connect in-person through a business networking environment such as a BNI meeting, conference, or panel presentation.

LinkedIn connections are very good for learning who is in your network as a "friend-of-a-friend". When we understand that most jobs, business opportunities, relationships, and even marriages begin through a "friend-of-a-friend" we realize how valuable this external network can be for us. You may connect in-person through tools such as references, introductions, or mutual friends via phone or e-mail.

Twitter connections are very good for seeking out others who share your interests. The "Advanced Search" function is an excellent tool for identifying individual "tweets" made by people talking about the same keywords you use. Business card exchange is a similar way to broadcast your message; however, Twitter does have an additional level of search to encourage specificity. The equivalent of this kind of search is like the difference between sending a general mailer to all doctors in the United States vs. handing out your business card to Phoenix-based radiologists who also happen to be graduates of the University of Arizona. In the case of Twitter, keyword search narrows the available options for you.

Tip 14
How to Treat People Online and Offline

Respect is key.

Treat others as you would like to be treated.

Make sure to mention others who are allies, friends, or supporters of yours.

Say THANK YOU as often as you possibly can. People like to feel recognized, and a declaration of gratitude goes a long way to increasing positive feelings.

Display an interest in the projects and endeavors of others in your social network. Each of us likes to feel needed, and each of us is on a unique path to explore our gifts and talents in the world. Use your social profiles to highlight the work of others within your network.

Be brave, thoughtful, considerate, and courageous when sharing what you need to share. Offline, people have the same feelings as they do online. Respect others, care for them, encourage them, and say thank you. All of us benefit from this behavior.

Tip 15

Pinging the People in your Network

All of your contacts within your network benefits from a periodic "reaching-out" to connect. You "ping" someone by getting in touch once in a while. I typically like to connect with a short note or e-mail every few months. Each response helps me keep my internal database of contacts up-to-date and it also gives me a good sense of what is going on in my associates' lives.

If you find that you are unable to "ping" people on a regular basis, consider at least contacting them twice or three times a year. You want to maintain a sense of connection and support. Infrequent contact is difficult for someone with a "loose" tie to you, as they may not remember you. Strive to connect once every few months: for example, once on your friend's birthday, once for Thanksgiving, and once in a general Spring e-mail.

Many marketers suggest you connect every 6 weeks, but I don't recommend this due to overall fatigue and over-use of advertising, spam e-mail, and e-newsletters. Connect on a regular basis and be personable. Don't overstay your welcome and make your "visit" short, sweet, and to the point.

Summary to Keep in Mind:
Etiquette and Maintenance

In general, demonstrate graciousness, calm, steadiness, and support to your growing network of fans, friends, followers, and connections.

There is no need to be hyper.
There is no need to be an ongoing commercial.
There is no need to be overwhelmingly chatty.

Use your social networks the way you would use the phone or e-mail. Consider reaching out on a regular basis, but schedule out your online "visits" so time passes and you may always assure yourself of a fresh welcome.

Know that each individual in your circle requires respect. You have an opportunity to show how much you value your connections by treating each person in your circle with respect, gratitude, and integrity.

Fill your relationships with others with respect.

Be fair.

Share what is most unique about you.

Celebrate our shared humanity. All of us are individuals and we treasure the unique connections that rise in their own special ways.

Many of your friends, associates, and potential customers benefit from an ongoing relationship with you, which comes from time, patience, and the ongoing "feeding" of that relationship.

While you may maintain an overall database of contacts, always make sure that someone on your mailing list has a way to contact you directly and receive the same kind of graciousness, care, and interest that you would provide on a one-to-one basis.

If you do have a large mailing list, consider pruning it by requiring confirmation from people. If someone truly does resonate with you and their message, they'll keep in contact with you. It is better for you to have 10,000 committed fans and followers than it is for you to contact a million people who won't even open your e-mail.

Chapter 5:
Expanding your Network

Cultivating your Community

What does it mean to connect with others? We started growing a home garden in 2004, and I always find myself becalmed, amused, enthusiastic, or otherwise emotionally involved with the plants.

I believe we develop similar connections with the people in our lives: we tend our connections, feed them and water them, and then we find and enjoy a rainbow of beautiful variety through our cultivated contacts.

Finding unity within diversity is our task, and when we make close connections with people, we start the continuous cycle of growing our circle of friends, refining and fine-tuning our relationships, growing our connections, and constantly displaying gratitude for those in our lives.

Consider your social networking efforts like you would consider gardening -- just a few minutes every day mean an ongoing harvest of beauty, nourishment, and connections.

Tip 16
Planting:
Growing your Social Network

Let's talk about relationships and how they impact your life and your business. Have you done an assessment lately of the types of people who are affecting you?

When you think about it, three different types of relationships are going to have an impact on your life:

1) positive relationships, such as friends, family, significant others, mentors, and associates, and people to whom you have a strong positive reaction

2) negative relationships, such as difficult clients, people who are mean, hostile, or malicious to you, challengers, and people to whom you have a strong negative reaction

3) neutral relationships, with whom you do not have a strong emotional connection

Also consider breakdowns from the above: you might know "friend-of-a-friend" people (easily found through a tool like LinkedIn.com), people who are interested in you (such as followers through Twitter.com or fans on Facebook.com), and regular friends with whom you share a mutually beneficial and positive relationship.

The task ahead of you is to identify your most important business relationships -- these "core" relationships will help you build your business. For example, some important business relationships will be your referral partners, such as companies that operate in a similar, allied industry to yours: printers and graphic designers are a close match, as are yoga practitioners, nutritionists, and acupuncturists.

Relationships take time and trust. Consider what your current relationship circles look like and where you can improve, because hundreds of thousands of dollars may be exchanged based on the strength of your relationships.

My list of people I relate to is the following:

- Experts: people who perform at a level I'm interested in
- Influentials: people who teach me by their example
- Mentors: my coaches and teachers

- Friends: from childhood through adulthood
- Work Associates: people with whom I've worked at other jobs
- People I'd Like to Get to Know Better

Who's on your own list of relationships?

In general, I advise you to move closer to people with whom you "resonate" with-- these are typically people on your "positive" list. I also advise you to reduce your exposure to people who are on your "negative" list.

Relationships are your key to growing your social network. As you increase and grow your professional profile, come into contact with more people, and interact with more and more people on a regular basis, you'll utilize tools like e-mail lists, Facebook, and phone calls to keep in contact and build your relationships.

Consider what your relationship circle for you and your company looks like in 5, 10, or 20 years. Act as if that circle already exists and believe that the types of relationships you're now fostering will be the strong relationships that carry you through your next levels of growth.

Tip 17
Tending:
Fostering Relationships

Your best-case scenario is a committed customer base with fans who buy your every product, spread the word about each of your new endeavors, and evangelize your service to friends, neighbors, and relatives.

How do you meet that special fan? How do you cultivate that ideal client? How do you "sort" the right people for your business from the wrong people for your business? How do you foster mutually beneficial relationships?

For all of us, it is easy to find the "right" people based on the kind of language we use and our own stated mission, vision, values, and philosophy.

Some ways to cultivate strong relationships include:

Say Yes to Only the Right Projects
Strengthen your resolve in saying "no" to the wrong projects so you can say "yes" to the right projects.

If you continue to say "yes" to the wrong projects you:

1) Have difficulty in discerning the quantity and quality of your projects
2) Become anxious, unfocused, unclear, and resentful
3) Lead by example: your "wrong" customers begin to ask for anxious, unfocused, unclear, and unfair requests

Create a niche and dominate it by saying yes to only the projects, distributors, customers, partners, or affiliates that match who you are, the community you want to build, and the goals you want to achieve. Populate all your social networking tools with stories of the clients to whom you have said "yes."

Narrow your Focus
Narrow your target market and narrow the type of work you do. Instead of doing "anything" or serving "anyone," specify you will only do something that you can become an expert on, or you will only serve a particular type of customer. Instead of working on "any project," promise yourself to work only with partners and clients who

intend to grow their business in a way that mirrors your own philosophy for growth.

With experience, you develop a better sense of intuition for when you are a good fit for a project or when you would rather refer the customer to someone who would be a better fit. In your social networking, feel free to "say no" by turning down invitations or friend requests from people who do not fit what you offer.

NOTE: In LinkedIn, just "archive" an invitation request, as a user with too many "I don't know this person" responses gets penalized. In Facebook, merely press "Ignore" if you do not want to become friends. In Twitter, you may "Block" a user if their profile is not a good fit for your reputation.

Be Efficient

As you develop a set of methods and stated business processes, you'll help everyone involved with your business. Think of your management and staff, your teammates, partners, and customers -- how does your process "fit" everyone's desired results?

If you haven't yet begun, start to use ongoing evaluation and guidelines to help you make decisions. A "decision tree" and a clear sense of roles and responsibilities becomes necessary so the most relevant individual responds to any incoming requests. When you emphasize efficiency in your company's decision-making, you give all the people working on your project a clear road map to milestones on the path to your shared success.

As an example of efficiency, use scheduling to manage your social networks:

- On Monday, I pre-populate some tweets on my chosen keywords to display throughout the week.
- On Tuesday and Thursday, I write my blog posts, making sure that they feed to Twitter using Twitterfeed.
- On Wednesday I review LinkedIn group discussions.
- On Friday, I check Facebook requests, wall posts, and messages. Pacing is everything.

Specify, Specify, Specify

Describe your business in 7 seconds or less. Be specific. As you specify what it is you value, you find people who share your values and who want to support you. You'll gravitate towards your "true community" of customers and partners.

For your social media outreach, keep on topic always. While it is tempting to start to become responsive, do as much as possible to be proactive, positive, and engaging. As an example, in my own blogging, I consistently focus on success stories rather than focusing on the many obstacles in the world. The way I see it, a reader can get information on obstacles and failures at another site, but on my site, we'll read about what I want to talk about: success, women, technology, and green businesses.

Envision the Future -- and Create it

Consider what your successful business looks like. I encourage you to map out what your company looks like in as much detail as possible, writing it on a piece of paper, or using vision boarding to copy and paste images that match your ideal.

Bring your current situation closer and closer to that ideal by saying YES only to the people and projects that match your vision. What will happen is the ideal starts coming closer and closer to you, and you do more and more of the work you love. As your company thrives and supports others who share your values, your entire community, society, and planet will benefit.

Use your social media profiles to enable connections between people you want to support. Consider offering connections between people you admire. Consider also offering a periodic "recommendations list" of people pulled from your list of associates, followers, fans, and friends.

Share your Voice

We all need your unique voice. We need you to share how you believe in your actions and how your work is a part of the solution. Share your unique vision of what it is you want to accomplish with your life, and let us all work together to make it a reality.

Ongoing reminders through your social outreach force you to act, live, and think in alignment with what you are posting. Post often on the types of topics you desire to see discussed.

Cultivating your Relationships

As you develop mutual relationships with others within your social network, it will become quite natural for you to grow these relationships. You find yourself surrounded by people who like and respect you, and who you like and respect.

To continue growing your relationships, we recommend constant dialogue, discussion, idea-sharing, and engagement. Ask your customers what they'd find useful and beneficial. Ask your partners and suppliers how you may help them.

Invite select customers to events, or offer customer-only benefits such as gift certificates, bonuses, referral fees, or members-only discounts.

Find ways to engage your community of clients and build your fan base through their efforts. Invite feedback and suggestions on how to improve your process. Consider integrating a constructive criticism evaluation form so you know what your customers think about your products and services.

As a reminder, always, always remember to say thank you.

Tip 18
Pruning:
Refining your Search

Consider for a moment what your ideal social networking circles allow you to do. With care and selection for the types of relationships you build, you find yourself making time for:

- Close, loving relationships with family
- Enthusiasm and support from close friends
- A supportive set of business associates
- The ability to to donate to organizations that you want to support
- The ability to share your knowledge
- Abundant quality time with loved ones
- The knowledge that you create a positive change in the world based on the way you run your business
- The thrill of connecting your customers with each other
- The opportunity to be a resource to people who need your assistance
- An increase in your ability to make dreams come true, for you and for others

‣ Spiritual development as you empower yourself and others

‣ A changed world, with more positive energy, more vibrant opportunities, and more ways for more people to participate

‣ An opportunity to increase in love and decrease your fear

All of the above are within your reach because they are the fruits of an active network of people who work together online and offline. However, being able to say "yes" to all of the above means being able to say "no" to opportunities, projects, and people that do not fit. You must take out your garden shears and prune the overgrown weeds and straggly bushes.

For example, if you are committed to a more healthy lifestyle, you must spend less time with someone who encourages you to eat junk food, or who pushes candy on you, or who invites you to imbibe detrimental substances. You might have to cut out, or prune, that relationship for a while.

You may have to say **no** to someone who does not support your vision for your life's work. You may have to "unfriend" or "unfollow" or "block" someone who does not share your passion. You may have to ban someone from receiving your messages.

What these drastic types of "pruning sessions" bring, however, is an increase in the circulation between you and your different social "branches."

By turning certain people or invitations down, you will find even more unique options cropping up, opportune circumstances arising, and newly positive occasions unfolding for you to get closer to your ideal situation.

Review some of the names on your "Contacts" list. Identify half a dozen names who no longer fit your sense of having a shared vision and passion. Perhaps they have said something, or done something you find does not overlap with your vision of the future. Perhaps they have acted in a way that doesn't resonate with your own character. Consider pruning as a way to increase your list of "cultivated contacts", or people with whom you have an active involvement. I promise you'll find five new people who enter your life to bring you closer to your mission, vision, and stated values. To increase your chances, start using people search or a topical keyword search to identify, read about, and connect with other people who share your passions.

Tip 19

Harvesting:
Saying Thank You

When you develop an attitude of gratitude, it becomes easy for you to say "thank you" to those who help you. When we harvest from the abundance of the garden, we are able to enjoy and share the fruits of our labors. When it comes to social networking and its impact on your business, remember to always incorporate a moment of gratitude and a way to say "thank you" directly to the people who help you.

Here are some ways to express your gratitude:

1) Share something of yourself.
Through your business, you are truly fulfilling the statement "Work is love made visible" by Kahlil Gibran. Your work is something that you share with others who truly benefit from your knowledge and skill. Approach your networking with this in mind -- you truly reach out to others who will help you and who you will help. Share freely of your gifts and you'll find many opportunities coming back to you.

2) A journey of a thousand miles begins with a single step.

Going into business is sometimes overwhelming for people: they get overwhelmed by the myriad of details needed, or they don't think they will get everything done. You will do it! Share your journey through your blog, website, and social networking profiles by explaining case studies, offering examples, sharing your research, introducing key players in your field, and going into depth about your industry or your specific process.

As you share the success of your efforts, invite others to become a part of your efforts -- you will find your customers becoming more engaged with you and more committed to your success.

3) Your company is an extension of your values.

Many successful women in business mention how important it is for them to use their business to fulfill their values. When you speak about values and integrate your values statement into your company's purpose, mission, and actual business practices, you provide a way for people to connect with you. Focus your efforts, and consumers will look to your business to provide leadership in your field of interest.

For example, it's important to me to increase the level of social and environmental responsibility that my company shares with our partners and customers. Through a sense of shared responsibility I envision a safe, clean, and prosperous future for all of us on our shared planet. This was important to me when I got started in business, and sustainable business practices continue to be integrated into our contracts, customer service, and delivery.

4) You have the opportunity to touch so many people.

Many of us fulfill a leadership role in our community. Because of your existing networking efforts and because of the many people that your products and services serve, you expand your personal reach and you are able to communicate, connect, and inspire many others.

Consider how your products and services impact your local community -- literally make a list and post it publicly. Your local clients, your customers in other states, and the people worldwide who use your products and services will be able to find you through your shared values and support your mission by aligning themselves with you.

For example, if you operate a green business, if you sell "green" products, or your business offers a green alternative to a conventional service, encourage all your customers to consider the net effect of their purchase with you. Your clients feel good about supporting your values through their purchase. Blog about your work and network online and offline with other green women in business, and you'll find yourself in the midst of a movement.

Publicizing your efforts is a great way to increase awareness of, exposure to, and knowledge of the issues you want to change.

5) Keep hope always in your heart.
Your biggest challenge is to manage your cash flow, find investors including yourself, and develop a system or product that makes your business procedure work.

Giving thanks to those who support your efforts takes the form of public statements, personal messages, and in-person connections. Keep a spirit of hope and a can-do attitude throughout your company, and you'll have an opportunity to bring on staff and customers who share your attitude -- be grateful in public and in private for these opportunities.

Tip 20
The Cycle Continues

We never know the net impact of our decisions. However, your efforts in the world have a chance to be amplified by others who share your commitment.

When you build your network, you meet specific individuals who put you into contact with their own community members. Like ripples in a pond, your mission reaches across multiple groups of people to stir even greater involvement.

Ways to increase the "cycle time" of finding new people to work with in a mutually beneficial matter include:

a) using specific search terms
b) using an "invite" feature to engage people
c) finding individuals within a specific region
d) asking trusted contacts for introductions
e) taking time to build up relationships
f) creating many opportunities for involvement
g) going outside your regular "circle" of acquaintances to reach new places and people
h) creating a discussion circle with others
i) creating mentorship relationships with new or junior members of your community

Networking means reaching out across our inter-related web of relationships to work together. Find people you resonate with, and work as a team.

There is no need for you to "go it alone," especially when there are other people who have skills that you do not currently have on staff, or when someone else has knowledge that you have no way of knowing. Your task as a leader is to identify your existing strengths and weaknesses, then use the social networks at your fingertips to meet and find others who complement your existing skill-set for your desired project, company, or business opportunity.

Checklist for your connections:

☐ What are your existing strengths? What strengths are already well-represented on your team? What are your existing weaknesses? What weaknesses do you want to overcome?

☐ Describe the type of person you'd like to meet.

☐ Consider your specific region: who do you want to reach, in what areas, to expand your ability to get things done? Think big.

Summary to Keep in Mind:
Expanding your Network

Expanding your network is a full-time job in itself, but you'll find that having the right people in your circle will help you accomplish things with more ease and in a faster time frame.

Consider growing your network like you would approach growing a garden. With consistent planting, pruning, tending, and harvesting, you have the makings of a group of individuals who share an interest in a common cause. Your web outreach efforts serve as an organizing tool to connect and focus people's efforts -- use all the tools available to you.

Remember that people appreciate when you recognize their efforts. Create opportunities to express your gratitude to those who create the most impact on your company.

People to give thanks and public appreciation to include your customers, your partners and suppliers, your staff, and those who have demonstrated a clear commitment to your company's success.

In your overall web strategy, consider creating easy ways for your web users to publish your marketing message. For example, you may want to come up with quizzes, graphics, badges, company information, a news feed, a Facebook application, or a mobile application. Some ideas:

- Consider publishing a YouTube series
- Invite your community to post reviews on Yelp!
- Invite your customers to upload a picture of them using your product and tag it with your company name on Flickr
- Offer a regular Delicious "roundup" of links that are tagged with your specific keyword or motto.
- Host a Twitter contest
- Offer your Facebook Fans a special discount
- For new visitors to your mailing list, offer something valuable as a download
- What can you give as a freebie, swag bag, or promotional item? Send it to your MySpace friends

Whatever the context, come from the position that your company desires growth and success through sharing and collaborating with others.

Chapter 6:
Measuring Data

How to Inform your Decisions

A social networking return on investment does not come with a hard-and-fast equation to tell you how to measure your success. Typical measures may not be valid when it comes to a genuine customer relationship.

It pays for you to begin with the end in mind. If you're starting a social networking effort, consider what numbers you want to measure, and what the expected change is as a result of your outreach efforts.

Consider your efforts in the social networking sphere to be part of your branding package -- use metrics to help you understand how you present your company and your services within the larger marketplace of buyers and sellers in your industry.

Ideas include average transaction per new customer, number of subscriptions to your e-newsletter, or number of signups to your mailing list. Additional ideas include rate of re-tweet (how many people repeat your message), number of fans and followers, number and quality of commenters, and unique visitors to your website.

Tip 21
How to use Metrics

We recommend Google Analytics as your base measuring tool. Some hosting packages also come with existing site visitor meters. Sign up for an account and embed the snippet of code generated into the footer pages of your website. When a visitor comes to the page, your analytics software tags their IP address, country of origin, keywords they used to come to the page, length of time spent on your site, and other data points.

We suggest you analyze a baseline report before starting on your social networking outreach efforts, then fine-tune your monthly or weekly report to understand the correlation, if any, between your social outreach and your website visitors.

Most tools allow you to cross reference the "conversion" rate of any of your efforts. For example, direct visitors to a specific call to action page (such as "signup for our package"). When your visitor signs up and receives a confirmation page, your analytics software has the ability to count how many people finished up at the confirmation page.

Tip 22
Understanding your Data

It may take a few weeks to understand your data. Particular pieces we point out include:

1) **The keywords your website visitors use**. Your web visitor uses certain keywords or phrases that lead them to your pages. Expand your page meta description and keyword tags based on these reports.

2) **The specific pages your guests visit.** Make sure there is a call to action on the top ten pages that your website visitors "land on." Understand why certain pages receive more views than others.

3) **The time users spend on your site.** How long are visitors staying with you on your online home? Consider lengthening your "About" section, providing more free information, or offering downloadable case studies or more in-depth articles to increase your visitor "stickiness."

4) **Frequency of visits per user.** How often do your visitors return to your site? With a small,

but excited base community, you have a built-in recruitment tool to spread the word about your products and services. Refresh your content to produce regular visitors.

5) **Pages per user.** Depending on your model, you may want a highly targeted base of customers visiting multiple pages within your site, or you may want multitudes of visitors checking one or two pages and leaving. Measure your data to understand how many pages a typical user visits.

Your web analytics gives you an excellent sense of how to better organize your sitemap of web pages and maximize your visitor's ability to gain the information they need.

Establish a sense of orderliness, trust, and communication through each part of your website. For example, offer fixed navigation and a prominent "About" page. Put your contact information on every page. Offer a "FAQ's" page. Consider adding extensive biographies of staff. Offer in-depth project case studies. Give your visitors what they need and they'll respect you and trust you.

Summary to Keep in Mind:
Measuring Data

With an initial idea of what your company considers to be a successful social networking plan, you can collect and report on pre- and post-campaign measures.

Typical outcomes relate to the overall standing of your company. For example, this might be an increase in the name recognition of your company within your specific niche, or it might be an increase in knowledge of your brand, or it may be an increase in the perception of the company, or an increase in fan-submitted user mentions related to your company's mission, vision, and values.

Consider the data points you would like to collect, and target this data collection on a regular basis. Weekly reports are targeted by Google Analytics: use the data generated from these reports to fine-tune your campaign and correct the course on your approach.

Data is a constant in the fluctuating world of the Web. Use your data to measure your success.

Chapter 7:
Final Tips

▸ Additional Expert tips

▸ 23. Begin with the End in Mind

▸ 24. Honesty is the Best Policy

▸ 25. Collaboration and Competition

▸ Summary to Keep in Mind: Your Social Profile
  Builds your Business

Additional Expert tips

In the following tips, we outline some additional ways for you to make the most of your social networking outreach.

Remember that social networking is but one path out of the many avenues of publicity open to you. Consider your Facebook, Twitter, and social media strategy as one part of your overall marketing and public relations plan.

Social networking
Blog mentions
Guest articles
Trackbacks
Links
Mentions (use Google Alerts)
Re-tweets (count from Twitter)
Links clicked (using a tracker tool, e.g. bit.ly)

Radio
Print
Television
In-person connections
Store visitors
Promotional events

Tip 23
Begin with the End in Mind

When you come up with a plan and your metrics for how you constitute the success of your plan, you have a roadmap to follow. With no plan or metrics, you have less information, followthrough, or purpose to the types of posts you create. If you decide to engage with social networking, what would be a good outcome?

▸ If you have an organization that's established, consider using these channels as additional ways for you to connect with your community.

▸ If you are working with a startup, consider your social networking strategy to be an easy way to find a first group of people interested in your message.

▸ If you're with a more experienced organization, consider utilizing social networking to enhance your website traffic, build your list, create a core group of clientele, and extend your ability to share your message.

Develop your plan, and stay on track with it.

Tip 24

Honesty is the Best Policy

Consumers want to know the "real" you. They want to know if they can trust your company. They want to know if you provide quality, and if you are able to help them with their needs.

Consumers want the truth. They want transparency and they require honest answers. There have been many cases of companies and organizations "getting it wrong": from jumping on questionable and/or offensive Twitter hashtags to display commercial messages, to hiring "fake" video bloggers, to distancing themselves from consumer complaints.

You want your customers to be your biggest supporters. You want your staff to be loyal and true to their work with your company. How do you do this? By being honest.

Come up with company policies. Engage with your customers, suppliers, and employees and encourage them with guidelines on what is acceptable to share in the social networking sphere and what is not acceptable. Post these prominently.

Commit to being as honest as possible. If you hide, dissemble, or deny the truth, it eventually will come out and you'll have double the duty to win back your reputation. Be honest in your dealings and do the right thing in real-time. If there is sensitive information than cannot be shared, at least mention that your company is aware of the issue and is working on a solution.

Post frequently. Your community of clients wants to know that you are available. They may not want an e-mail newsletter every week, but if they visit your Facebook Fans page, they like to see that you have something available for them, like an image, a video, an employee story, or a coupon.

Admit your mistakes. To err is human. Build a stronger group of fans by engaging with your people and letting them know when you've made mistakes and what you're doing for course correction. Make things right. Refrain from blame or shame: move forwards.

Appreciate others. Say "thank you" to those who find errors or product flaws. You have many people available to help you make your product or service better. Express gratitude when they are willing to help you.

Tip 25
Collaboration and Competition

We live in a world of increasing collaboration, more competition, and a higher expectation of transparency, trust, and excellence. My best advice for you to achieve success in your organization is to make sure that everything published resonates with your stated mission, vision, and values.

Relationships are built around common values, so as you become more and more clear about your market niche, it will be easier and easier to find partners, publishers, and affiliates.

- Build your Twitter following through guest blogging, pro bono work, or through group efforts that promote your Twitter handle
- Build your Facebook "Friends" list through personal friends and recommendations
- Build your Facebook "Fans" page through adding a signup link on all your web properties
- Build your LinkedIn profile through one-on-one connecting: make connections with people through Groups

Summary to Keep in Mind:
Your Social Profile Builds your Business

We recommend you keep an ongoing, personalized relationship with your customers. Your most valuable relationships come from fans and customers who are engaged with you, who recommend you to their friends and family, and who are willing to call you, tweet you, post you, and share your links.

Your personal efforts magnifies your overall company-wide effort: as a representative, or "ambassador", you offer a personalized window into what it is like to work for the organization. Potential fans are the ones interested in the "behind-the-scenes" functioning of your company.

Understand what would internally constitute a successful metric for your outreach, and use that guideline throughout your social strategy.

Keep honest in all your publications. Honesty really is the best policy.

In unity, find diversity. Share as much as possible (within company guidelines) and personally invite other people to join your cause.

CONNECTION
=
GOOD

(courtesy of 10K Webdesign)

Conclusion

My overall goal with this book and others in the A Successful Woman's Handbook series is to provide you with targeted resources as you build your organization. I recommend "Fifty-one Ways to Build your Community of Clients Online" http://www.tinyurl.com/51ways if you are considering building a website or desire enhancements to your existing website.

Any endeavor benefits from the care and feeding you put into it. With time, attention, continued maintenance, and a true spirit of connection, your social networking efforts will serve you well.

Please visit me online at my own company, www.10kwebdesign.com where we design and build websites for membership groups, green businesses, and progressive organizations.

I also invite you to join me at my community, www.ASuccessfulWoman.com. On this member-supported site, I offer additional resources, information, and tools. I've implemented a forum section for peer-to-peer discussions and news sharing. I also screen different services, review books, try new products, and provide free articles that share much of my experiences with success thinking and business building. If you would like to share your own business resource for other success-oriented women, please contact me for inclusion on A Successful Woman.

If you are a representative from a "green" or earth-friendly and sustainable company, please list your business for free on the directory at my newest endeavor, http://www.GreenBizWomen.com. I look forward to connecting with you.

> Here's to your success!
> Monica S. Flores

Resources

- Facebook
- LinkedIn
- Twitter

Facebook

Facebook is no longer the province of Gen-Y'ers. Your boss, associates, and most of your high school graduating class are probably there, too.

As the 400,222nd user on Facebook: http://www.facebook.com/profile.php?id=400222, I've become much more active in the last year. Here are 20 tips I've learned that will help you make the most of your "Facebook Experience."

One of the beauties of the Facebook environment is that you get what my friend Allen Gunn has referred to as an "ambient knowledge" of the status of your friends, through their "status updates." You may also use Facebook to post or trade notes, connect with others, share interesting items from your web searches, and generally keep abreast of new developments in your friends' lives. Facebook is particularly good for finding people with whom you haven't connected in a long time. I've found long lost elementary and middle school friends here, and some of them are now turning into business associates and partners.

Any working woman knows the benefits of an expanded network. Facebook is a great tool because it has birthday reminders, the ability to "group" friends, and e-mail facilities. Your Facebook profile is a public way to share who you are. Use it wisely!

Tip 1) Logging in. You'll have to log in if you want to be a part of Facebook. Choose an e-mail address that you regularly check and a password that you'll remember.

Next, you'll organize your profile, edit your "Info" section and then connect to, or "add as friend," people who already are on Facebook.

Tip 2) Keep your information private. Once you're logged in, go to the top right: Settings (next to Logout) and change your PRIVACY Settings, particularly your Profile (your "presence" on Facebook)

http://www.facebook.com/privacy/?view=profile

as well as your News Feed and Wall

http://www.facebook.com/privacy/?view=feeds

You may specify what you'd like to share on publicly-available "feeds" (on your friend's homepages) here.

Tip 3) Update your info. Edit your Education Info and/or Work Info as you like. You may also use a little box under your picture for your motto, your business information, a quote, or something creative.

Tip 4) Smile! Your Profile Picture is the way you show who you are. Most people either display just their own face (better), or a picture with their family (a little more difficult to see).

Tip 5) Find people you know. To find people you know, go to:

http://www.facebook.com/srch.php and do a search by a person's name or e-mail address, a classmate search, or a company name search. Once you get some search results, review them. If you click "Add as Friend," they will get a notification and either Confirm or Ignore your request to add them.

Alternatively, "Send a message" to that person without adding them to your "Friends List."

They'll receive your message in their Facebook e-mail inbox.

Tip 6) Find more friends. There is a "Friend Finder" to help you find people you e-mail if you use gmail, hotmail, yahoo, or other web-based mail services.

http://www.facebook.com/findfriends.php?ref=sb

Tip 7) Your "Wall" is public. Use it! The "Wall" is a publicly available location where people post things like notes, images, videos, and your status update. Other people may post to your wall and you may post to others' walls.

Tip 8) Share your Photos. You can easily upload photos using your "Photos" tab.

Tip 9) Use your status update wisely. Your status update is the box "What's on your mind?" It may be used for many things besides sharing what you are doing.

Use it to share links, ask questions, or post photos or videos. Use www.tinyurl.com if you'd like to take a long website link and make it shorter.

Tip 10) Specify, specify, specify. If you are using your social network for procuring products and services or marketing your own, consider putting your keywords and phrases into your "Info" tab, under the "Personal Information" section. Then, these will appear in the general Facebook Search function.

When someone types your particular key phrases into the Facebook Search function, your listing will appear. For example, one of my key phrases is "minority women in business."

Tip 11) There are two main feeds, a "Status Feed" and a "News Feed." If desired, you may create a new customized group of friends, and their feeds will be posted to your customized "Group" feed.

Tip 12) Customize your homepage. If you find that your Facebook homepage is being dominated by certain people, control if you want "More" or "Less" about that particular friend. On your "Home" page, a little to the right of an item within your "Feed," move your mouse around until you see "Hide" and then click to hide that particular friend's posts.

Tip 13) Control e-mail notifications. If you find that you are receiving too much e-mail from Facebook, based on activity on your profile, edit your e-mail notifications.

Go to "Settings" (top right, in between your name and "Logout")

From the dropdown menu, choose "Account Settings."

Go to "Notifications." This is where you may specify what types of e-mail you allow Facebook to send you.

Tip 14) Organize your "Friends" list. You have the option to group your friends into different friend lists. Click the Friends link on the top left navigation menu.

On the left-hand side is a link to "Create New List." Give the list a name you'll recognize, then type in the names of friends. When you receive new-friend requests, you may add them to a particular list.

Tip 15) Start or join a group. From the left hand sidebar section of your "Home" page, you have an opportunity to set up new groups -- look for the "Groups" tab. You may have to expand your list of displayed items.

A group in Facebook is just like a group in real life—a gathering of people interested in a particular idea, issue, or cause. Use the Search bar to find thousands of different groups that have been set up for different interests. You can locate mine by searching on, "A Successful Woman."

Tip 16) Discuss amongst yourselves. Within groups, you may participate, follow, or review different topics for discussion. Note that each discussion topic is also viewable in search engines, so refrain from posting private information like e-mail addresses.

Tip 17) Facebook for Business. The "Pages" section is a great way to promote your company or business.

http://www.facebook.com/business/dashboard/?ref=sb

If you are an official representative for your company or brand, you may set up a page about your business and recruit fans to that page. It's a nice addition to your website or blog, and you'll have the opportunity to send messages to all fans when needed. If you are an administrator for the page, Facebook allows you to purchase advertising and view pageview statistics.

Tip 18) Facebook knows people you may know. When you first log on to your "Home" page, there is a little section on the bottom right-hand side that lists "People you may know." The social search mechanism identifies potential friends for you based on your mutual friends. If you see someone you recognize and know well, consider clicking "Add as Friend."

Tip 19) Share it. Typically, there is a "Share" button somewhere on the pages within Facebook. You can use that link to quickly post something to your own "Wall," or to send to someone in your network via Facebook e-mail.

Tip 20) About applications. Applications are add-ons offered by companies and individual developers. Be CAREFUL. Use your best judgment when installing applications, as they are often big time-wasters, or involve major time commitments (I usually click IGNORE this application). Some applications share your private information on Facebook with other applications from other website developers. Be mindful of what gets posted on your profile by you and by others.

Finally, the silhouette of a head that shows up in the bottom right hand corner of your Facebook window is part of the Facebook chat bar, which allows you to participate in real-time chats with friends. You can always "Go Offline" to hide yourself from chats.

Bonus recommendation: Fix a certain amount of time that you'll focus on the Facebook part of your online social networking and STICK WITH THAT TIME allotment.

Here's to the great connections you'll make on Facebook!

LinkedIn

LinkedIn.com continues to grow. This is such a beneficial tool for online networking, and I continue to use it for strictly business use. As of October 2009, the site had more than 45 million registered users spanning 150 industries.

If you do not yet have a profile, it's worthwhile to review the components of a complete one.

These include:

1) a picture
2) a list of past positions (including titles, dates, and responsibilities) and your current job or position
3) a "summary" of your achievements
4) educational history
5) list of links (such as a link to your company, your blog, your personal website)

Here's my own profile for your review:
http://www.linkedin.com/in/monicaflores

From LinkedIn directly: "Since, like in the real world, the size of your network on LinkedIn depends on the number and quality of connections you have, we recommend you have at least 20 connections to people you know and trust on LinkedIn. You can do the search above with fewer connections, but you'll get fewer and less meaningful results. Use the following link (get logged-in first) http://www.linkedin.com/pymk? showMore= to find your existing contacts on LinkedIn in less than two minutes."

If you already have a user profile at LinkedIn, consider these ways to maximize your profile to directly translate to more business, a better quality of business, a list of better testimonials, more detailed information and research, and the like:

1) Keep your connections updated. Many users of LinkedIn sign up and then do not utilize the site's capability because they do not maintain their lists of connections. I keep a link to my profile in my outgoing e-mail signature and I consistently connect with clients, customers, associates, and confederates through my business. Each connection typically yields more connections based on mutual friends or opportunities to meet others. Use this technology to increase your own "yield" of connections.

Many connections = many opportunities. Few connections = few opportunities. When you use the tool to connect with people you know, like, and/or trust, you'll have a better quality of connections and a better "feel" for what is happening within your network.

2) Publish your content. If you have created items like blog posts, Powerpoint presentations, or Amazon reading lists, LinkedIn now allows multiple options to "post" this information to your profile. Think of your LinkedIn profile as a quick way for a potential partner, researcher, employer or customer to get a "view" of what kind of person you are. The publishing aspect of LinkedIn offers another avenue for you to demonstrate your expertise.

Note that LinkedIn will publish, as part of its default options, all of your changes. Check in the "Settings" section and check items such as notifications, what you want the LinkedIn network to do, and how you want your profile details to display. https://www.linkedin.com/secure/settings?trk=hb_acc (for logged-in members only)

3) Answer questions. If you are knowledgeable about a particular field, share you knowledge in the "Question and Answers" section on your LinkedIn homepage. Questions may be broad and generalized

or micro-specific and niche to your industry. If you have a question about a particular idea or item, share it here too. You have the opportunity to present your skills in your chosen field: use it.

4) Connect with specific individuals that you seek. LinkedIn has an ability to browse the profiles of people at the specific companies or at the specific level of work you seek. Are you a job-seeker? Consider doing a "search" on the job position you desire and location you desire to see a list of people in that situation. You may then contact them using LinkedIn's version of e-mail. This may work for you to find people with whom to conduct an informational interview, or for people with whom you would like to establish a relationship.

5) Testimonials count. While it's considered "tacky" to directly solicit testimonials, many people do use their profile to demonstrate their expertise by posting recommendations received from their connections. Testimonials may arrive from partners, former bosses or clients, associates, or friends. Consider that you can also write your own testimonial about someone else you highly recommend.

6) Join a group. Multiple groups covering all topics and issues exist on LinkedIn. You may use the group affiliation (which displays on your profile) to share your values, connect with others who share your interests, and keep abreast of discussions within your community. For example, I am a part of my alumni group within LinkedIn, which is a great place to hear news and to "virtually meet" with other classmates.

7) Claim your profile and protect it. "Phishing" is the damaging task of spammers who harvest your personal information. The benefit of maintaining and managing your own account is that you claim your identity and no one else can pretend to be you and/or invite others based on your name. When you claim your profile, you may also link to that profile in places like your blog, company website, or other places you'll need some references.

Once you start to manage your social network, you'll see an increasing ability to meet others who will help you in your goals, whether that's increasing your reach, finding a new position, or meeting with others in your field.

Twitter

I believe Twitter helps your business by helping you connect with like-minded people.

Here are 20 of my tips on using Twitter:

1) Twitter is comprised of 140-character updates.

It's an excellent way to connect with other people who are interested in the same things you are. It is also an excellent way to have a search-engine friendly "micro-blogging" tool. It is free and easy to use.

2) Following.

The difference between Twitter and Facebook is that you may "follow" someone else, but they don't have to "follow" you back. (In Facebook, when you "friend" someone, they automatically "friend" you back.)

The difference between Twitter and LinkedIn is that Twitter is more of a blend between personal, social, and business, and can be more anonymous/username driven, while LinkedIn is business-related, formal, and connected (you use your real name, and you know a connection, or you know them through someone else).

3) Twitter is a conversation.

Twitter is a way to connect with other people. Treat it as such. Refrain from being to "sales-y" or worse, connecting with no one, only talking about yourself, or marketing yourself as a Twitter expert.

4) The homepage.

When you login within Twitter, you may also "follow" anyone else: such as a person, organization, brand, or company. Anyone may "follow" your account, which means your postings show up on their homepage.

5) To begin, set up your account.
http://www.twitter.com
Your username such as a shortened version of your business website, or your own name will be good. Note that the "handle" is usually @somethinglikeyourname, so for example, I am @monicadear and found here: http://www.twitter.com/monicadear.

The number of characters in your handle counts towards your total of 140 characters, so make it short if you can!

6) Reserve your account names.

You may consider "storing" versions of your long name (e.g. I have also reserved my full name and I point people back to my active account) as well as your company name (we have another Twitter account that's only company-related).

If possible, add a direct link to your Twitter feed from your live website, and add your company website to your Twitter profile page, to confirm that you are the legitimate owner of the account.

Your Twitter homepage is
http://www.twitter.com/youraccountname

7) Settings.

Once you're logged in, go to the "settings" page to set up your website URL link and your bio.
http://twitter.com/account/settings

Do you want to get an e-mail notification whenever someone starts following you?
Set your notifications here:
http://twitter.com/account/notifications

Upload a photo of yourself for personalization.
http://twitter.com/account/picture

Use Twitbacks.com if you'd like a free way to personalize your background. Or, ask your graphic designer to customize your background.
http://twitter.com/account/profile_settings

8) Time to start finding other people.
Go to: http://search.twitter.com and type in your key phrases. Mine are minority women business and here are the results for that search: http://search.twitter.com/search?q=minority+women+business. Try the search on your own keywords (like your industry, your interests and hobbies, your business specialization, etc.)

Click on anyone's name to see their profile page.

9) What to post?
You'll notice that most new Twitter postings start out with regular status updates (like what someone ate for lunch, where they're commuting to in their car, if they're at the airport). This is a fairly typical starting point: most first posts by Twitterers have these mundane items.

What's better is to start posting directly and specifically on your key phrases and asking questions, connecting, and networking based on your interests.

10) When you click on any Twitter username, you land at their profile page.

You may click the "Follow" button under the name to start "following" that person's updates. If they have the option set up on their own profile, they'll receive an e-mail that you started following them.

11) Connecting.

As you start to find people you like or if you're looking to connect with others, you may use the "What's happening" box to send that person a message. You do so by adding an @ in front of their name, and then sending a message (within the 140 character limit). So, for example, on your homepage, to send me a message, you would write:

@monicadear Here is my message and I thought the Social Networking book was great!

12) Your username in the Twittersphere.

If anyone writes you in their message, you may see the "mentions" by clicking on the @username link on your right-hand sidebar:

13) Tagging others.

You may tag multiple people in your message, such as:

@10kweb @monicadear I liked the book, it was such a fantastic resource.

Then, all the people with the @ sign will receive the mention of your message.

14) Direct messaging.

Now that you're connecting with people, some may "follow" you back. If so, you may "DM" or direct message them. You do this by typing into your box:

dm monicadear this is a direct message to Monica to say how much I enjoy Twitter

A direct message is more like a personal e-mail and doesn't show up in the "twitterstream" of items on your homepage. It shows up in the "Direct Messages" folder on your Twitter homepage.

You receive an e-mail if someone direct messages you, if you've turned "on" that notification in your profile settings | notifications page.

15) Trending.

Trending topics, meaning "mentions" of a topic, now show on the right hand sidebar. To comment on a topic, you add the hash tag and the one word name of the topic, like so:

#followfriday or #ecomonday

Twitter is a source of immediate information on many topics. The search engine within Twitter is now also starting to check regular words and phrases, so the hashtag solution may start reducing in importance.

16) Set-aside codes.

There are some interesting set-aside codes in the Twitter "What are you doing" box that may be helpful.

For example, write: whois username, where username is the Twitter username, click update, and you'll receive a brief summary of that person:

whois monicadear

17) Advanced search.

In search.twitter.com, you may use the Advanced Search features to find posts on a specific topic or keyword, or by a specific person.

You could also use the following codes:

near: to find any tweets posted near a particular city, such as

fashion near:Los+Angeles

or within: to find any tweets posted within a certain radius of you, such as:

women in business within:15mi

18) Quality versus Quantity.

Everyone wants more Twitter followers, it's a fact.

That said, it's my belief that you will reach more people, and be more effective and spreading your message, by building real relationships with others. This is social networking, after all. Give me one good friend, or give me ten good-hearted and kind individuals who connect, communicate, and care —

I don't need a thousand people who don't care and won't do anything when I ask them for help.

19) Realtime communications.

Twitter is an excellent place to get immediate feedback, kick around ideas, and receive answers to your questions... right now.

Consider it like a search engine on real people in real time with real responses, immediately. Businesses have been using it to post Twitter-only deals, to connect and provide a "voice" to the consumer, to answer customer complaints, and to give news as it happens.

For my web design business we typically embed the latest tweets into our clients' website pages. You can find more about widgets and badges here:
http://twitter.zendesk.com/forums/10711/entries/15354

20) Different ways to access your account.

Many Twitter users migrate to a different application or platform (phone, Blackberry) to manage their tweeting instead of logging on to the Twitter.com website directly.

For example, I periodically use TweetDeck.com, an installed application, to manage my "tweets." You may also bypass your machine and use your mobile phone.

Mac and iPhone users may consider Twitterrific.

Twitpic allows you to share photos directly to Twitter.

I also use Twitterfeed.com, which takes posts from your blog and automatically "feeds" them to your Twitter account.

You can see many more applications here: http://twitter.com/downloads.

Some people use Twitter to update their Facebook status (which may be helpful to you, if you don't regularly log in to Facebook).

Connections

I invite you to connect with me directly.
You may find me through a search on "monicadear".

Here are some other places around the web where you may learn more about me:

Facebook: monicadear
http://www.facebook.com/monicadear

Facebook Group: A Successful Woman
http://www.facebook.com/group.php?gid=8098862349

Facebook Fans: A Successful Woman
http://www.facebook.com/pages/A-Successful-Woman/42863436442

LinkedIn: Monica S. Flores
http://www.linkedin.com/in/monicaflores

Twitter: monicadear
http://www.twitter.com/monicadear

Additional links include:

Delicious: monicadear
http://www.delicious.com/monicadear

Friendfeed: monicadear
http://www.friendfeed.com/monicadear

Slideshare: monicadear
http://www.slideshare.net/monicadear

Flickr: monicadear
http://www.flickr.com/photos/monicadear

Pandora: monicadear
http://www.pandora.com/people/monica151

YouTube: monicadear
http://www.youtube.com/user/monicadear

Yelp: monicadear
http://monicadear.yelp.com

Recommended Websites

Women in Business
http://www.womenonbusiness.com
http://www.asuccessfulwoman.com

Green Women in Business
http://www.thegreengirls.com
http://www.greenbizwomen.com

News
http://www.google.com/alerts
(to set up an alert specific to your interest)

Content Management Systems
http://www.joomla.org
http://www.drupal.org
http://www.wordpress.org

Domains and Hosting
http://www.10khosting.com
http://www.godaddy.com

www.ingramcontent.com/pod-product-compliance
Lightning Source LLC
Chambersburg PA
CBHW072047190526
45165CB00019B/2069